# Jesus: The Word of God

# Jesus: The Word of God

## MARGARET O'TOOLE

Published in North America by
The Liturgical Press, Collegeville, Minnesota

ISBN 0-8146-2235-6

First published 1992
Designed by Tom Kurema
Cover design by Tom Kurema
Cover Jisas Krais, by Kuage
Reproduced with permission of Godconcepts Collection

Typeset by Collins Dove Desktop Typesetting
Printed in Hong Kong by HarperCollins*Publishers*

Every effort has been made to contact the copyright
holders of illustrative material. The editor and publisher
apologise in those cases where this has proved impossible.

The Scripture quotations in this publication are from the
New Revised Standard Version of the Bible, copyrighted
1971 and 1952 by the Division of Christian Education of
the National Council of the Churches of Christ in the USA.

Nihil Obstat: Rev. Brendan J. Hayes, L. Eccles, Hist.
      Diocesan Censor
Imprimatur: Rev. Monsignor H. F. Deakin, Ph.D.
      Vicar General
Date:     15th January, 1992.

The Nihil Obstat and Imprimatur are official declarations
that a book or pamphlet is free of doctrinal or moral error.
No implication is contained therein that those who have
granted the Nihil Obstat and Imprimatur agree with the
contents, opinions or statements expressed. They do not
necessarily signify that the work is approved as a basic text
for catechetical instruction.

# CONTENTS

# 1 INTRODUCING JESUS, THE WORD OF GOD

*You will conceive in your womb and bear a son and you will name him Jesus.*
**(Luke 1:31)**

*And the Word became flesh and lived among us.*
**(John 1:14)**

*'And the Word became flesh and lived among us.'*
(John 1:14)

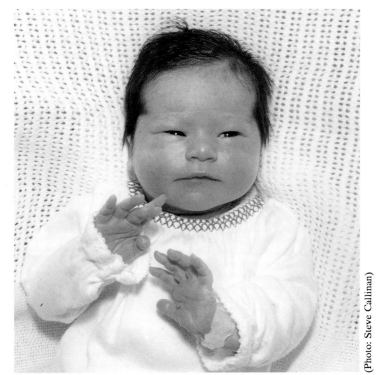

(Photo: Steve Callinan)

1

This is a story about Jesus, who is the Word of God. We call him by many names:

*Jesus Christ*
*Jesus of Nazareth*
*Son of God*
*Son of Man*
*The Messiah*
*Emmanuel*
*Son of David*

In the Hebrew language the name Jesus means 'saviour'. The Hebrew way of saying the word Jesus is Yeshua. That is what Jesus' family and friends called him.

Jesus is his God-given name. It is the name that the Angel Gabriel told Mary to give him when God sent Gabriel to ask her to be the Mother of Jesus. The name gives us an important clue about who Jesus is and what he would do during his life.

*'But WHO is Jesus?'*

But WHO is Jesus?

This is THE GREAT QUESTION—one of the greatest questions that anyone has ever asked.

What do YOU think are some of the answers?

How much do you know about Jesus?

*Where was he born?*
*Where did he live most of his life?*
*What did he look like?*
*What did he do during his life?*
*What did he talk about?*
*Did he talk about God?*
*Did he have many friends?*
*What were some of the things he liked doing best?*
*Did he make many enemies?*
*Why did he die on a cross?*
*What did his friends say about him after he died?*
*Is he alive today in a special way?*
*Why is he so important to so many people?*

As you read this book you will find some of the answers to THE GREAT QUESTION: WHO IS JESUS?

*THE GREAT QUESTION: 'WHO IS JESUS?'*
(Photo: Luke Pellatt)

So…let's start looking for some answers. Where do we begin?

(Photo: Michael Trainor)

# 2 WHO IS JESUS? WHERE TO FIND SOME OF THE ANSWERS

*[Jesus] asked them,*
*'But who do you say that I am?'*
**(Mark 8:29)**

T he first and most important place to look for answers to THE GREAT QUESTION: WHO IS JESUS? is in four different books called the Gospels.

## What is a Gospel?

Some time after the death of Jesus his followers realised that he was risen from the dead and was still with them in a very real way. They were able to realise this because of the great power of the Spirit who had come upon them at Pentecost. The coming of the Spirit made a very great difference in their lives. Most of these followers of Jesus were Jews, but as time went on people who were not Jews also came to believe in Jesus. People who are not Jews are called Gentiles.

The people who believed that Jesus was risen from the dead gathered in different people's houses to share their memories of him—to remember what he had said and what he had done during his life. They wanted to understand the importance of the things Jesus said and did before he died. They shared their stories and broke bread together as a lasting memorial of Jesus present among them.

*'They went to many different Jewish, Greek and Italian towns to tell other people...*
(Photo: Ancient Greece. The shops and Temple of Apollo, by D. & J. Heaton, Scoopix)

These people went to many different Jewish, Greek and Italian towns to tell other people about Jesus and his importance for everyone on earth. They believed that through the person of Jesus God had spoken all that God wanted people to know and understand and do in order to live their lives in the best possible way. They gathered as a group—or perhaps several groups—in different cities in Asia Minor, Greece and Italy, especially in Rome. Each group was called a 'household group', and eventually became known as a 'church'.

They believed that Jesus was now with God, and they began to give Jesus the title of Christ. This title meant that Jesus was the 'anointed' One of God. In the centuries before Jesus lived, the Jewish people believed that God would one day choose someone to carry out God's great mission on earth. That 'chosen One' was to be called 'the Christ' or 'the Messiah'. The Christians soon believed that Jesus was the chosen One. That is why they called him

Jesus, the Christ
Jesus, the Messiah

Soon the followers of Jesus were called Christians, because they believed that he was Christ, the chosen, anointed One of God.

As the years passed, the Christians were very anxious that the importance of the life of Jesus would not be forgotten. This made them decide to write down what Jesus had taught, and the stories of what he had done during his life. What they wrote down is now found in the four Gospels.

The Gospel according to Mark is most likely the first Gospel written. Mark probably wrote it about thirty-five years after the death of Jesus. We are not sure where Mark lived when he wrote his Gospel. What we are sure about is that he was concerned for the group of Christians—the church group—living in his own city, and about the problems they had in living the way of life that Jesus wanted. What Mark did, then, was to write down many things that the Christians in his city remembered about Jesus. These included some of Jesus' teachings; for example, some of the parables. As well, Mark gathered stories about what Jesus did, such as the miracle stories. Most especially, Mark gathered together many stories that tell of the events leading up to the death of Jesus on the Cross. He believed that these stories written in his Gospel would help the Christians in his church to make connections between the life and teachings of Jesus and the kinds of things that were happening to them in their lives.

When we read the Gospel according to Mark we can have some idea of what was happening to the Christians in Mark's church.

It is most likely that each church group made copies of Mark's Gospel.

*'…they believed that he was Christ…'*
(Photo: Graeme Horner)

About twenty or more years after Mark wrote his Gospel, three more Gospels were written. These are called:

The Gospel according to Luke
The Gospel according to Matthew
The Gospel according to John

Like Mark, Matthew and Luke and John wrote their Gospels for the Christians in their own churches. Like Mark, they used the stories about Jesus and his special teachings that the people in their own local church groups remembered. Like Mark also, Matthew, Luke and John were concerned about the special problems of their Christians and how the teachings of Jesus and stories about him would help the Christians in their own particular situation.

The Gospels of Mark, Matthew and Luke are called the Synoptic Gospels. This means 'seeing them together'. Matthew and Luke did not know that the other was writing a Gospel. Both of them had a copy of Mark's Gospel. They copied down some of the stories exactly as Mark had written them. But they changed some of Mark's stories in ways they thought would be helpful for their own Christians. Matthew and Luke added stories that we do not find in Mark's Gospel.

When we read Matthew's Gospel, we find that Matthew wrote about Jesus in a different way from Mark. And when we read Luke's Gospel we discover that Luke wrote about Jesus in a way that is different from both Matthew and Mark. When we 'see them together' we can tell what parts of Mark's Gospel were changed by Matthew and Luke to help their own Christians. This is why these three Gospels are called 'Synoptic Gospels'.

These three Gospel writers did not mean to write the story of Jesus' life *exactly* as it happened each day or each year. Instead, they wanted to help the Christians in their own church to know what Jesus did, and that he was still with them to help them in their daily lives. They wanted to link everything that happened in Jesus' life with what was happening in the lives of the Christians.

When we read John's Gospel, we find that it is very different from the Gospels written by Mark, Matthew and Luke.

John wanted to help his Christians in the same way that the other Gospel writers did. But he decided to write his Gospel in a different way. John chose just a few stories of important things that Jesus did in his life. For example, like Mark and Matthew, John wrote down the story of how Jesus fed five thousand people with five loaves and two fish. Then John did something different with this story. John wrote a good deal about how this miracle was really a *sign* that Jesus would continue to be with Christians in the Eucharist. He would continue to share his life with them to give them strength and nourishment in their lives as Christians.

John also wrote much about the teachings of Jesus and about the importance of believing that Jesus is the Word that God has spoken to everyone.

The word Gospel means Good News. The life of Jesus tells us that God has come into our world in a very special way, to help people to live better and happier lives. The life of Jesus shows us that even when we are sad or in pain or feeling lonely, God is very close to us at these times. That is why the Good News is so wonderful. Because of Jesus, we can believe that God can and will do wonderful things in everyone's life. Jesus tells us how a human person should live with others in order that everyone can live in love and peace. This was Good News indeed for the people in Jesus' lifetime, especially those who were poor, outcast and friendless. This Good News of God coming into the world in the person of Jesus is the main message that each Gospel writer wanted to tell everyone.

All the Gospels were written in the Greek language, because that was the language that people spoke at that time.

*Gospel means Good News.*
(Photo: Michael Coyne, Talent Bank)

Mark starts his Gospel by saying,

> *The beginning of the good news of Jesus*
> *Christ, the Son of God.*
>
> **(Mark 1:1)**

This is the 'beginning' of the Good News. The Gospels continue to be Good News for us today because we still need to learn what to do to live with other people in love and peace. When we read the Gospels carefully we can find out how this Good News helps us to be as good as we can possibly be.

The four Gospels tell us about WHO JESUS IS, but each one of them tells us about Jesus in a different way.

It is like having four different portraits of Jesus.

Mark's portrait shows that Jesus is a great Teacher and Miracle-worker. But Jesus is also the Suffering Messiah who reveals that being brave when we have pain is an important way of living our lives the way Jesus lived his life.

Matthew's portrait shows that Jesus is the One whom the Jewish people eagerly waited for. Jesus is the Christ, the Messiah, the Son of David, whose coming had been foretold many times in the Sacred Scriptures.

*'He is the One who is filled with compassion and love for the poor and the hungry, the outcast and all who suffer.'*
(Photo: Graeme Horner)

**11**

*In the beginning...*
(Photo: Helga Leunig)

Luke's portrait shows that Jesus is the Saviour, the great Healer. He is the One who is filled with compassion and love for the poor and the hungry, the outcast and all who suffer.

John's portrait shows that Jesus is the Word of God, the divine Son of God who has come down from heaven to reveal who God is for all people.

# JESUS IS GOD'S WORD

*In the beginning was the Word,*
*and the Word was with God,*
*and the Word was God.*
**(John 1:1)**

This is the way John begins his Gospel. Here he is calling Jesus the Word of God. What does this tell us about who Jesus is?

*First, we must think what a word is.*
(Photo: Graeme Horner)

First, we must think of what a 'word' is. When we speak words it is like telling our own secret knowledge or what we are thinking *inside ourselves* to other people who are *outside ourselves*. We *reveal* something of ourselves to another person. Some words that we speak are very important, and we do not forget them; nor do other people. For example, we can say the words 'I love you' or 'I think you are a great person' or 'I forgive you' to other people. When we speak these words it is like letting loose the *power* to love other people and to forgive them that is hidden inside us. Our words become like a *vehicle* to express what is hidden inside us. If we did not say these words, then other people would never know that this power to love them is inside us.

Words tell other people what we *want them to know* about us. We can choose to keep our thoughts about something well hidden away from others. But once we speak a word about something, then we have let others know what we are thinking, and we can never take our words back and pretend that we have never spoken them. Words, when they leave us, really have a life of their own. Once we have spoken a word, we cannot catch it and hide it back inside ourselves. Our word is there, outside us, and it can have great power to act on other people.

Very often we can tell *what a person is like* by the words that they choose to say. If a person generally speaks kind and happy words, then we know what kind of a person they are like inside themselves.

We know that the words we speak can have an effect on other people. If we speak angry words, then we can hurt others. Our words have the power to bring a response from another person. Our words can make other people happy or sad.

**14**

When a human being speaks a word:

- that word comes from deep inside them where it has been hidden away;
- that word lets loose a *power* like love or anger;
- that word can tell us what the other person *wants us to know about them*;
- that word has a *life of its own* away from the person who said the word;
- that word *does* something:  it has an effect on others;
- that word tells us *what the person is like* who speaks the word;
- that word makes us *respond* to the one who speaks it.

If this happens when a human person speaks a word, then how is Jesus the Word of God?

All through the centuries before Jesus was born, God spoke in different ways to many people, such as Moses, Samuel and the prophets.  The people of these early centuries believed that when God spoke, God's word actually made something happen.  For example, we read in the book of Genesis that God said, 'Let there be light!' It happened! The words of Genesis read, 'and there was light'.  God's word caused the light to come into existence.

When we call Jesus the Word of God, we are saying something very important.  We mean that at a certain time in history, when the reign of Herod the Great was coming to an end in the province of Galilee, God 'spoke' a final Word in the person of Jesus of Nazareth.  In Jesus, God said all that is needed for us to know about God.  Jesus is like the *vehicle* that explains something of the kind of great Being that God is.  Because Jesus is God's Word, God makes wonderful things happen on earth.

God has told us a great secret.  The way God told it is by way of the life of Jesus.  The way Jesus lived on earth, the way he died on

*God has told us a great secret.*
(Image: Gowrie Nyak)

the Cross, and through his rising from the dead, God has told us something that was *deeply hidden* inside God, something that we could never have known if God had not told us—if God had not spoken the Word, Jesus. Jesus is the Word that *reveals* to us what God is like right inside the very secret hiding place in God.

In Jesus of Nazareth, God has let loose God's *power* to be with human people for all time. Jesus has the power of God, because Jesus is God's Word spoken at a certain time in history and in a particular country called Palestine. We know from the life of Jesus that this is the power of LOVE.

When we read the Gospels and come to know the teachings of Jesus and the stories of what he did before he died, then we know what God *wants us to know about God.*

Jesus is God's Word spoken in a certain time and place. God will not take back that Word. That Word of God who is Jesus will always be with us. When we come to know *Jesus*, we will always be able to know *what God is like.*

When we read the Gospels we know that Jesus did many things. He brought dead people back to life. He cured the sick and gave sight to those who were blind. He befriended the poor and anyone who was outcast from society. The Gospels tell us that Jesus taught people the best way to live a human life. Because Jesus is God's Word, we know that God was *doing all of this* in Jesus. Jesus as the Word of God speaks the Good News that God wants us to know. And the Good News is that God loves us more than anyone could ever love us and is always with us no matter how hard life can be.

During his life Jesus had a powerful effect on people. After he died and rose to new life, this power continued in the lives of the Christians. They *responded* to the Word of God spoken in Jesus and lived their lives according to the teachings of Jesus.

Human words reveal who we are and what we are really like inside ourselves.

God's Word is much greater than our words. God's Word is the actual person of Jesus.

To listen to Jesus is to listen to God speaking.

To see what Jesus does is to see what God does.

This is why we call Jesus the Word of God.

**17**

*Palestine in the time of Jesus.*

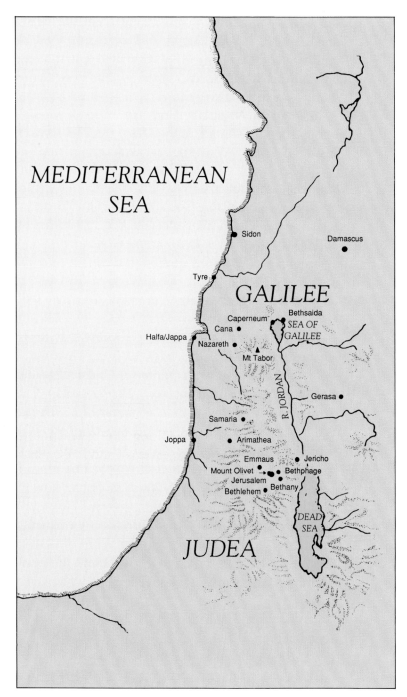

# THE PLACES WHERE JESUS LIVED

*In the time of King Herod, after Jesus was born in Bethlehem of Judea*
**(Matthew 2:1)**

*When he came to Nazareth where he had been brought up*
**(Luke 4:16)**

We know from Matthew's and Luke's Gospels that Jesus was born in Bethlehem. When he was still a young child, Mary and Joseph went to live in Nazareth. This is where Jesus grew up. Bethlehem and Nazareth are both in Palestine.

Palestine is a long, narrow country, bordering the Mediterranean Sea. It is about 250 miles long and between 30 and 50 miles wide. Along the Mediterranean sea-coast and in the north of the country the land is green and fertile. Farther inland there is a ridge of rocky hills and mountains, and beyond that there is a very wide flat valley that is mostly desert. Through this valley the river Jordan flows south until it enters the Dead Sea.

Although it is a very small country, Palestine has always been very important, because it is where three continents meet: Europe, Asia and Africa. Anyone can go by land from Europe to Asia to Africa through Palestine, so Palestine is an important trade route for sending goods from one continent to another. For this reason many nations have conquered Palestine at different times in its history. About 300 years before Jesus was born, a great Greek leader called Alexander the Great conquered Palestine. Then about 60 years before Jesus was born the Roman armies arrived in Palestine and conquered it

*The Gospels tell us that it was in the hills of Galilee that Jesus lived most of his life—*

*Sea of Galilee and Horns of Hattin today.*

(Photo: Michael Trainor)

completely. They were still in control of the country when Jesus was born.

Even though the Greeks did not keep control of Palestine, they did bring to the country many aspects of the way they lived in Greece. They brought with them their learning and art, their trade and form of government, and especially they brought their language to Palestine. Even though other countries conquered Greece, these countries did not destroy the Greek language and culture. So Greek remained one of the languages spoken in Palestine, although it was probably only in the trading cities that it was commonly spoken. In the country parts and in the hill towns, particularly in Galilee, people continued to speak their own language, which was called Aramaic, and to follow their own Jewish religion and culture.

*Miracle of loaves and fishes.*
(Image: Gowrie Nyak)

In the time of Jesus, Palestine was divided into three different parts. The southern part was called Judea. Here was the main city of Jerusalem. Farther north was Samaria. The people who lived there were called Samaritans. They were a Semitic people who traced their history back to Abraham. The Jews in the rest of Palestine did not like the Samaritans. They thought the Samaritans were not true Jews, and that they were not as good as the Jews in the rest of Palestine. North of Samaria was Galilee. The Gospels tell us that it was in the hills of Galilee that Jesus lived most of his life. There were many towns that had fishing industries centred around the Sea of Galilee. Some of these towns were Capernaum, Bethsaida, and Chorozain, and the Gospels name them as some of the towns where Jesus went to teach the people.

The different kinds of land in Palestine affect the weather. In most parts, except for the inland desert, it is hot and dry in summer and cool and wet in winter, something like the weather in parts of Australia. Often, strong winds would sweep down from the mountains and cause a sudden storm over the Sea of Galilee. So Jesus would have felt the great heat of the summer months as well as the cold wind and rain of winter.

Because Jesus came from Nazareth, many called him Jesus of Nazareth. Nazareth was a small village, where most of the people were peasant farmers or trades people; for example, Jesus belonged to the trade of carpentry. He was a craftsman, so he did not belong to the poorest groups of people in Palestine.

We know from the Gospels that Jesus went to many towns and country areas, teaching people about God and working many miracles. Although he travelled mostly around places in Galilee, he went to Jerusalem several times. It was just outside Jerusalem that he died. Occasionally, he travelled beyond the borders of Palestine, but for most of his life he stayed in and around Galilee. Jesus walked most of the time from place to place. There were many times when he was tired, dusty and thirsty.

Because he spent most of his life in Galilee, Jesus spoke in the Aramaic language. He might have known a little Greek, and he could read and speak the Hebrew that was found in the Hebrew Scriptures.

*'he spent most of his
life in Galilee…'*
(Photo: Michael Trainor)

*'I was sent only to the lost sheep of the house of Israel.'*
(Photo: Michael Trainor)

# 5 JESUS WAS A JEW

*[Jesus] went to the synagogue on the Sabbath day, as was his custom. He stood up to read the scroll of the prophet of Isaiah.*
**(Luke 4:16–17)**

Jesus was not a Christian: he was a Jew. Mary, his mother, was a Jew, so Jesus would have looked like her and like the other Jews living in Nazareth. Most likely he had dark hair and olive skin and was probably not very tall. His parents, Mary and Joseph would have taught him how to pray the Psalms, which were the special prayers of the Jewish people. They would have brought him to the synagogue in Nazareth. He would have learned the teachings of the Torah, which is the Law of Moses written in the Sacred Scriptures. The Torah also includes the traditional ways the Law of Moses was interpreted.

(Photo: Shirley Politzer)

25

God gave the Law to Moses many centuries before Jesus was born. The Law was one of the most important parts of the Jewish religion. Jesus lived a very holy life. He knew that God had given the Law to Moses. He obeyed God when he followed what God wanted him to do in keeping the Law.

Jesus prayed to God many, many times during his life. Sometimes he spent the whole night praying to God. He did all that he was supposed to do in order to be a good Jew.

We know that when he was grown up he went to the synagogue many times to pray and to read from the Hebrew Scriptures. He also went to the Temple in Jerusalem to celebrate the Jewish religious feastdays, such as the Feast of Tabernacles. He celebrated the Feast of Passover in Jerusalem just before he died.

When we read Matthew's Gospel in particular we find out that Jesus mixed mostly with Jewish people. It was mostly Jewish people Jesus taught and healed. Of course, Jesus became very famous, so people who were not Jews came to ask for his help. We know that a Roman officer asked Jesus to cure his servant (Matthew 8:5–13), and a poor woman who was not a Jew, but a Canaanite, asked Jesus to cure her daughter, who was in the power of a demon (Matthew 15:22–28). Jesus healed the sick servant and drove out the demon from the poor woman's daughter because the Roman officer and the Canaanite woman had great faith and really believed that he could heal sick people.

> *Just then a Canaanite woman from that*
> *region came out and started shouting,*
> *'Have mercy on me, Lord, Son of David;*
> *my daughter is tormented by a demon.'*
> **(Matthew 15:22)**

As a Jew, Jesus belonged to the chosen people of God. These people were called the Israelites. The religious story of the Israelites went back for nearly two thousand years before Jesus lived. During that long story the Israelites believed that God was always with them to guide them and look after them. But something new began to happen with Jesus. Jesus began to understand that when *he* taught the people in the villages and in the countryside and when *he* healed their sickness, God was continuing to look after the Jewish people through what *he* said and *he* did. He believed that God had sent him to teach the Jewish people especially.

*He believed that God had sent him to teach the Jewish people especially—Jews today at the Western Wall.*

(Photo: Michael Trainor)

The followers of Jesus called him 'Rabbi', which is a special kind of Jewish teacher. Jesus did not belong to the Jewish priestly class of people. To be a priest a Jewish boy had to be a member of one of certain families. From the Gospels we learn that during the lifetime of Jesus there were three main groups of Jewish religious leaders. Jesus often had strong arguments with them, and some of them became his real enemies.

The three main groups were called:

> *the Sadducees,*
> *the Pharisees,*
> *the Scribes.*

Most Sadducees belonged to the Jewish aristocratic families and were included in the priestly and non-priestly classes. They were the religious leaders of the people of Palestine, and so had a lot to do with the Roman rulers and were friendly with them. The ordinary people of Palestine did not like the Romans, and so they did not really trust the Sadducees to be on their side. The High Priest for the Temple came from the Sadducees.

The word Pharisee means the 'separate one' or 'holy one'. Pharisees were laymen who obeyed the Law of Moses as exactly as possible, and they studied it very carefully. They believed that the thing that pleased God most was being faithful to the written and traditional Law of Moses. They believed that the Jewish people were a holy nation and should apply the Law to every detail of their daily lives. They did not like sinners, tax-collectors and any other people who did not keep the Law strictly. They thought that all these people, because they did not keep the Law of Moses very well, could not be close to God: this really meant most of the people of Palestine. The Pharisees did not like the Romans and would not co-operate with them as the Sadducees did.

The main task of a Scribe was to define the precise meaning of the Law. He became a disciple of a rabbi when he was young, so that he could learn to interpret the Law. Because Scribes were important people in government and in education, some of them thought that they were superior to others. They wanted people to think they were better than other people. They often wore special clothes so people would recognise them and think that they were very important. In Mark's Gospel, Jesus warns his followers not to be like the Scribes.

> *As he taught, he said, 'Beware of the scribes, who like to walk around in long robes, and to be greeted with respect in the marketplaces, and have the best seats in the synagogues and places of honour at banquets!*
> **(Mark 12:38–39)**

The first followers of Jesus were Jews also. After the death and resurrection of Jesus these followers continued to live as Jews. Every Sabbath they went to pray in the synagogues. They also began to meet in houses to remember Jesus and to break bread together. They continued to keep the Law of Moses. It was not long before there was a separation between Jews and other people who were not Jews but who wanted to follow Jesus. When we read the Gospels, we can tell that this was a great problem for those who wanted to be faithful to Jesus.

John in his Gospel tells us that a number of people, especially from among the religious leaders, refused to believe in Jesus. When John wanted to say who these unbelievers were, he used the word 'Jews'. Of course, John did not mean *every* Jew; but all through the centuries after Jesus' life, many Christians did not understand this. They blamed *all* the Jews for not believing in Jesus. Most important of all,

*Seder meal in a Moroccan Jewish family.*
(Photo: Michel Hayaux duTilly)

many Christians blamed *all* the Jews for killing Jesus. Some Christians believed that the Law of Moses was no longer important for anyone, even for the Jewish people. They also thought that the Jewish religion did not matter any more because Jesus had come to teach us and to save us. They said, 'Only Christianity is important now!'

Maybe this is a reason why many thousands of Jews have had to suffer all through the centuries since the time of Jesus.

Because Jesus was a Jew, the Christian religion is very closely connected to the Jewish religion. This is something we must keep in our minds all the time.

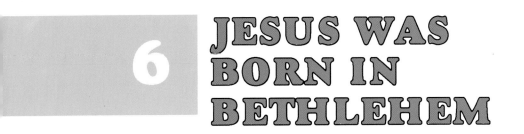

# 6 JESUS WAS BORN IN BETHLEHEM

*And she gave birth to her firstborn son and
wrapped him in bands of cloth, and laid him
in a manger…
But the angel said to them…
I am bringing you good news of great joy for
all the people…*
**(Luke 2:7,10)**

We celebrate Christmas by remembering the stories
found in Matthew and Luke about the birth of Jesus.
Mark and John did not tell any stories about the birth.

*Adoration of the
Magi.*
(Peter Paul Rubens,
1577–1640)

**31**

Every year at Christmas time we remember Mary and Joseph coming to Bethlehem. We remember that Jesus was born in a stable, and was wrapped in swaddling clothes and laid in a manger. We sing carols about the angels announcing the birth of Jesus to the shepherds. We remember how the Magi came from the East to worship Jesus. When we hear the story of how King Herod tried to kill Jesus, we are glad that Joseph and Mary were able to escape into Egypt and that Jesus was not killed.

Perhaps we have never wondered *why* we have these stories or where they came from. Remember that the Gospel writers wrote their Gospels long after Jesus' own life. They wanted to help the Christians in their own church to understand the meaning of the teachings of Jesus, what he did, and what had happened to him in his life.

So why did Matthew and Luke write about the birth of Jesus? Luke and Matthew wrote some stories about the birth of Jesus, not to 'invent' Christmas, but to show how important the birth of Jesus was. They wanted the stories of his birth to be a kind of forecast or clue to point to what Jesus would be like and what he would do when he grew up. So the stories of the birth of Jesus were carefully chosen by Matthew and Luke to proclaim that right from the moment that Jesus came into the world he was the Saviour for whom the Israelites had waited so long. He was the chosen One of God.

Matthew and Luke wrote two very different stories about the birth of Jesus. They even seem to contradict each other. Luke writes that when Jesus was born, Mary wrapped him in swaddling clothes and laid him in a manger. Luke also tells of the angels coming to announce the Good News of Jesus' birth to the shepherds, who belonged to the Jewish people. Mary is an important person in Luke's story. She is the one who, even though she does not understand what God is doing in her life at this time, believes that God has a plan. So she trusts God completely, with great faith.

Matthew does not tell us about the stable or the angels or the shepherds. But it is Matthew who writes about the coming of the Magi from the East. These wise men belong to the Gentiles. When we put Matthew's Gospel with Luke's Gospel, we discover that they tell us that Jesus came to save all people: the Jewish people (that is the meaning of the shepherds in Luke's story) and the Gentiles (that is the meaning of the Magi in Matthew's story).

Matthew also writes that Herod, the King, tried to kill Jesus. Jesus escaped death when he was a child, but when he was grown up other kinds of rulers would put him to death.

Even though the Gospel writers wrote such different stories of Jesus' birth, they did write down some very important things about Jesus that are the same. This is what they both wrote:

---

- Jesus is the Son of God.
- Jesus is truly human. He was born like any other human.
- From the very beginning of his life, while he was still in Mary's womb, the power of the Holy Spirit was with him.
- Jesus is the chosen One of God. He is the Christ, the Messiah.
- Jesus is the Saviour. When he grows up, he will save people by forgiving them their sins, by freeing and healing them.
- He is given a special name, which means 'Saviour' (Luke) and 'Emmanuel', God-is-with-us (Matthew).
- Mary is his Mother, and she is a descendant of King David.
- Joseph is Mary's husband, and he also is a descendant of King David.
- Jesus was born in Bethlehem.
- Jesus was born in a time in history when the reign of King Herod the Great was coming to an end.

---

So we know now that Luke and Matthew wrote what we call Christmas stories. But we also discover that what they are really writing about is who Jesus is and what he is going to do for 'all the people' when he is grown up.

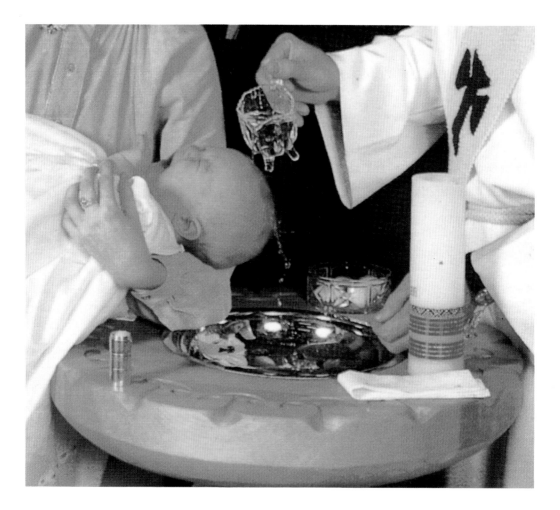

# THE BAPTISM OF JESUS — A SPECIAL TIME IN HIS LIFE

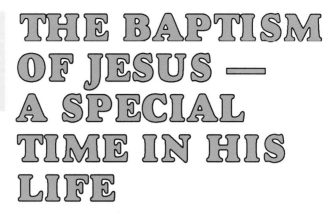

*In those days Jesus came from Nazareth of Galilee and was baptised by John in the Jordan.*
**(Mark 1:9)**

*And when Jesus had been baptised, just as he came up from the water, suddenly the heavens were opened to him and he saw the Spirit of God descending like a dove and alighting on him. And a voice from heaven said, 'This is my Son, the Beloved, with whom I am well pleased.'*
**(Matthew 3:16–17)**

All the Gospels tell us something about the baptism of Jesus, so it must have been a very important happening in his life.

One day, when Jesus was about thirty years old, he left his home and his family in Nazareth. This was the beginning of a new life for Jesus. He did no more carpentry work after that. He must have been wanting to do some special work for God. He began what we call 'his ministry'.

'*This is my son, the Beloved, with whom I am well pleased.*'
(Photo: Michael Trainor)

His ministry means the very special work that God wanted him to do. From the time he left Nazareth, until he died, he spent his time helping all the people who needed him. He spoke out against the rulers who made life hard for the poor people. He taught people about God, telling them how much God loved them and how God had opened the heavens and was with them to help them in new and amazing ways.

But before he began his ministry Jesus went down to the Jordan, where John the Baptist was preaching to many people who had come from the towns and countryside to be baptised. John the Baptist was a great prophet and knew that the time was very near for God to come into the world in this amazing way, in Jesus. John the Baptist wanted all the people to prepare for this great coming by asking God to forgive them for having sinned.

When Jesus came to the Jordan he stepped down into the water to be baptised. As soon as John baptised Jesus, something wonderful happened. The Gospel of Luke tells us that

> *... the heavens were opened, and the Holy Spirit descended upon Jesus like a dove. And a voice came from heaven, 'You are my Son, the Beloved, with you I am well pleased.'*
> **(Luke 3:21–22)**

Do you remember the reason why Matthew, Mark, Luke and John wrote their Gospels?

It was to tell the Christians how important Jesus was for them and for all people. They remembered what Jesus did and what he said and they wanted to explain the meaning of all this to the Christians.

So what was the special meaning of the baptism of Jesus?

Here are some answers.

The 'heavens' is where we say God is. So, if the heavens are 'opened', this is like a sign that there are no barriers between God and people any more now that Jesus is on earth.

The 'Holy Spirit descended upon him in bodily form like a dove'. This is the sign that God has specially anointed Jesus. It means that Jesus is God's favourite: the One God loves more than anyone else. It is also a sign that the Holy Spirit is with Jesus and will stay with him in a powerful way when he is doing God's special work in his ministry.

**37**

The 'voice from heaven' is a sign that God was speaking. It was as though God was pointing out Jesus to everyone and saying:

*Jesus is my beloved Son. I delight in him. Whatever Jesus says or does, pay attention and listen to him because what he does is very pleasing to Me!*

*'...pay attention and listen to him because what he does is very pleasing to me!'*
(Photo: Michael Trainor)

We might wonder why the Gospel writers used the image of a dove when they wanted to tell us about the Holy Spirit coming on Jesus at his baptism. Perhaps one reason could be that the Israelite people believed that a dove was a sign of love. There were many rabbis whose teachings had been written down. This is called the 'rabbinic tradition'. In their teachings the rabbis wanted the people to know how much God loved them. Sometimes they said God loved the Israelites so much that they were like God's favourite.

Matthew, Mark and Luke probably knew the teachings of the rabbis. But they wanted to say that it is now *Jesus* who is God's favourite. God delights in Jesus because Jesus is the one who begins a new friendship between God and all people, both Jews and Gentiles. Through Jesus everyone can now be God's favourite.

That is what the 'voice from heaven' says at the baptism of Jesus.

And that is why the Spirit has the form of a dove at the baptism of Jesus.

After his baptism Jesus began to think very deeply about his special mission. Was God now sending him out to all the towns and countryside to tell people how much God loved them and how much God wanted to help them?

The Gospels tell us that after his baptism Jesus went out into the desert wilderness by himself to pray to God and to think very carefully about how he would live his life so that he would obey God. While he was there, the devil tried to tempt him to turn away from his decision to love God above all else and to turn away from doing what God wanted him to do. This was like a battle between the power of Jesus and the power of evil. We know from the Gospels that the power of Jesus was far greater than the power of evil. Jesus won this battle and sent the devil away. After forty days in the wilderness he came back to Galilee. He had made his decision to begin his ministry.

When Jesus was baptised, he was truly anointed. What happened at his baptism was a sign that God had anointed him for a special mission, to be the one to *reveal* God to all people. Jesus is God's Word, telling us who God really is.

In Luke's Gospel we read that when Jesus came back from the wilderness he went into the synagogue in Nazareth on the Sabbath. This was his Jewish custom. He was given the book of the great prophet Isaiah to read. And when he opened the book he found the place where it was written

*The Spirit of the Lord is upon me,*
*because he has anointed me to preach good*
*news to the poor.*
*He has sent me to proclaim release to the*
*captives*
*and recovery of sight to the blind,*
*and to let the oppressed go free...*
**(Luke 4:18)**

This is exactly what Jesus is going to do for the rest of his life!
This is why he was anointed at his baptism!
This is why he is Christ!
This is why he is the Messiah!

- He will preach the Good News to the poor.
- He will release all those who are captive to illness or fear or worry.
- He will cure all kinds of blind people.
- He will help all the people who are crushed and oppressed.

Do you remember what the name Jesus means? It means Saviour. A saviour is a person who rescues anyone who is in trouble. During his life Jesus did many things to rescue people who were in all kinds of trouble and under all sorts of oppression. That was his special mission. That was his ministry.

So Jesus is the best possible name that anyone could give to him. The name of Jesus is a wonderful clue to tell us who Jesus is.

And what happened at his baptism is another great clue. Now we know that Jesus is God's Son. God points to Jesus and says:

*'Look at what Jesus does!' 'Listen to Jesus!'*
*'I am very pleased with him because when Jesus speaks—from now on—then I am speaking!'*
*'When Jesus does great things for other people—from now on—then I am doing them!'*

Jesus' baptism is the beginning of the most important part of his life. Much more will happen to him that will help us find out who he is.

*Jesus' baptism is the beginning of the most important part of his life.*
*Much more will happen…*

(Photo: Tricia Confoy)

*Believe in the Good News!*
(Photo: Helga Leunig)

# 8 JESUS PROCLAIMS THE KINGDOM OF GOD

*Jesus came to Galilee, proclaiming the good news of God, and saying, 'The time is fulfilled, and the kingdom of God has come near; repent, and believe in the good news.'*
**(Mark 1:14)**

What did Mark write down as the very first words that Jesus said to begin his ministry? The first words that Jesus said at the beginning of his ministry were (according to the Gospel of Mark): 'The kingdom of God has come near: repent, and believe in the good news.'

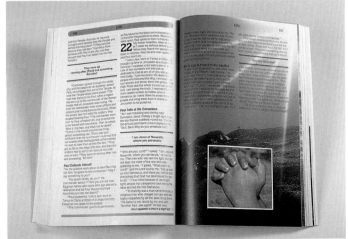

(Photo: Bill Thomas)

The Kingdom of God!

All the Gospels tell us that this is the central message of Jesus during his ministry. Jesus proclaimed that God's loving rule over people would destroy the rule of evil that was hurting people and making them suffer. The Good News is that the power of evil is destroyed by God's *power* in Jesus.

What does the Kingdom of God mean?

The Israelites called God 'Yahweh'. This was the special name God had told to Moses. It was the name God wanted the people to use when they spoke about God, or prayed to God. The Israelites had great hope in Yahweh. Yahweh had rescued them from slavery in Egypt. They believed that Yahweh would save them and give them fullness of life, freedom, peace and every blessing. This was one way they described the Kingdom of God that would come in the future.

The phrase 'Reign of God' is perhaps a better way of explaining the meaning of the Kingdom of God. Both phrases describe the ongoing actions of God present with people on earth to give them help to live better lives.

The word 'Kingdom' does not mean that God has a territory or land called God's Kingdom. That is the way we think about an earthly king having a kingdom. What the Israelites really meant was that God (Yahweh) had spoken to them through their leaders and had made a covenant with them. The covenant was like a sacred promise God made to the people. The covenant meant that God promised to be always with the Israelites, even if they turned away from God. As part of the covenant, the Israelites promised to obey God in everything they did. To accept what God wanted them to do in the covenant meant that they accepted the 'reign of God' in their lives. God was the Ruler or Sovereign of their hearts and their lives, and when they obeyed God they were allowing God to reign in their lives.

The Kingdom of God did not mean God's territory, but God's rule in the lives of people, and God's rule is always one of LOVE.

Jesus did not invent the idea of the Kingdom of God. He knew about it from his own Israelite religious history.

**44**

Jesus believed that this was the best image he could use to tell the people of *his* time that the long-awaited Kingdom or Reign of God was happening among them through what he would teach them and do for them. He did not believe the Kingdom of God was just one geographical space. He believed that the Kingdom of God meant that God was really helping everyone in their lives to fight against the forces of evil. It did not matter who they were. God wanted to help all people, because everyone was precious to God.

*He had great compassion for suffering people.*
('Boy in Street', painting by Robert Dickerson)

That meant that each person was precious to Jesus. What people remembered most about him was that he had great compassion for the suffering of people. He loved people and cared deeply what happened to them. He was a great friend to everyone, especially the poor and oppressed people. He challenged the rules of society, the government system and the religious rules, when these worked to make life hard for the poor and the outcast. He was always their greatest champion.

Jesus proclaimed two things about the Reign of God.

He told the people that God's Reign was happening in their lives each day. He encouraged them to hope in God more and to think about how God was with them every day to help them in their struggles. He was sure that God's Reign was already happening in their lives, because he was sure the Kingdom of God was happening in his own life in a very special way.

He also told them that God's Reign was coming in the future in a wonderful way. As a Jew, he looked forward to the future coming of God's Kingdom, just as all the other Jews did. But he believed more than any of the Jews that God was faithful to this promise. He told the crowds who gathered to hear him that they had to think very hard about what was happening in their everyday lives, because everything that happened to them was important, especially their sufferings. God would change the way people live human life and everyone would be given fullness of life, freedom, peace and every blessing in the future Kingdom.

When Jesus proclaimed the Reign of God, he wanted people to know that the reign of all forms of evil would be destroyed. The power of evil had ruled over the world. He told the people of his time that they had to repent and turn away from doing evil things. This meant they had to change the sinful ways they were living their human lives. He told this to the poor and the rich because there were sinful people in both groups.

Most of all, he told the rich and powerful people they had to change from committing sins that hurt other people. They had to stop using their power over poor people and stop making life hard for the poor. The powerful people had to stop thinking they were superior to anyone else. God loved *all* people. In the new Reign of God all people are equal and precious to God. The powerful could no longer treat other people as if they were worthless. They could no longer say that the laws that they made people obey were the most important thing in the world. Jesus continued to proclaim that in God's Reign, *people* are the most important. God's Kingdom is all about how people should live together, respecting each other and reaching out to stand up for others when they were in trouble or were suffering.

46

Jesus taught that in the Reign of God:

- To believe that God is very powerful and very loving is the most important thing that matters in anyone's life.
- Loving God and doing what God asks is the way to show that you belong to the Kingdom of God.
- The rule of evil in the lives of people would be destroyed.
- Everyone is to be included in the Reign of God: no one can be left out as if they do not matter.
- Everyone has the right to be treated with fairness, equality and justice. When this happens, then the Kingdom of God is visible for everyone to see.
- Everyone has a responsibility to look after each other, to have compassion on one another and care for anyone in need. This is the way to show that God's Reign is happening in the lives of people.
- Everyone is to make sure that people can live together in freedom and peace. These are the signs that the Kingdom of God is taking place in the lives of everyone.
- In the Kingdom of God the only thing that matters is that God loves everyone equally. No government or rule can be greater than that.

To live like this is to live Kingdom-life.

Many times in Israelite history special people called prophets had spoken out against the powerful rulers who made life hard for others.

Jesus spoke out like these prophets of old, but he was different from these prophets. What he said and what he did really made the Kingdom of God happen in the lives of people.

Everything Jesus did, such as the miracles he performed in driving demons out of people, or curing the sick and the crippled, or raising dead people to life, was real proof that God's Reign—God's powerful presence—was changing the sufferings of people and making their lives better. This is one way of saying that God, through Jesus, *saves* people.

Everything Jesus taught, such as his parable stories, his wise sayings and the great teaching of the Beatitudes, were very powerful teachings about the meaning of the Kingdom of God for all people.

Most of all, because he himself was the example of all that he said and did, he brought about the Reign of God in people's lives. He was so loving and compassionate to everyone; he treated rich and poor with respect and dignity; and had great courage to challenge the powerful leaders of his time in order to help those who were their victims.

It is no wonder that this was Good News. The Gospels tell us that the crowds were amazed when they heard what Jesus taught them, when they saw the wonderful miracles that he shared.

(Photo: Graeme Horner)

**48**

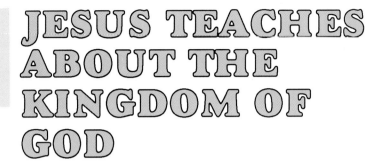

# JESUS TEACHES ABOUT THE KINGDOM OF GOD

**9**

*Jesus went throughout Galilee, teaching in their synagogues and proclaiming the good news of the kingdom...*
**(Matthew 4:23)**

*They were astounded at his teaching, for he taught them as one having authority, and not as the scribes.*
**(Mark 1:22)**

esus was a great Teacher. He used many wise sayings to teach the people about the Kingdom of God. The Gospel writers gathered these wise sayings of Jesus and wrote them down. They wanted their Christians to learn about Jesus from what he said. Here are some of the wise sayings of Jesus.

*For all who exalt themselves will be humbled, and those who humble themselves will be exalted.*
**(Luke 14:11)**

*Do not judge, and you will not be judged.*
**(Luke 6:37)**

*Forgive, and you will be forgiven; give, and it will be given to you... the measure you give will be the measure you get back.*
**(Luke 6:37–38)**

*But if anyone strikes you on the right cheek, turn the other also.*
**(Matthew 5:39)**

(Photo: Graeme Horner)

Jesus was also a great story-teller. The stories he told are called 'parables', and he used them to teach the people about the Reign of God. A parable always has an unexpected surprise hidden in the story. The parables Jesus told were about ordinary people, plants, food and things that his listeners knew about. When he included in his parable an unusual and extraordinary idea about these familiar things, it made people think hard about the *meaning* of the parable.

When Jesus wanted to explain to the people how the Reign of God, which was starting with him, would grow and spread across the whole world for all people to belong to, he told the story of the Mustard Seed. In Mark's Gospel Jesus says,

> *With what can we compare the kingdom of God, or what parable will we use for it? It is like a mustard seed, which, when sown upon the ground, is the smallest of all the seeds on earth; yet when it is sown it grows up and becomes the greatest of all shrubs, and puts forth large branches, so that the birds of the air can make nests in its shade.*
> **(Mark 4:30)**

In another parable Jesus wanted to teach that until the coming of the fullness of God's Reign in the future, the Reign of God in the present would be with the reign of evil in the world (Matthew 13:24–30).

In another parable Jesus wanted to teach the people how to act in order to belong to the Kingdom of God. Luke's Gospel is the only one that tells the beautiful parable of the Good Samaritan (Luke 10:30–37).

The story is about the traveller on the road to Jericho who is robbed and beaten and left on the roadside to die. Two people who were the official keepers-of-the-law come by, but do not help the man in case they would be made unclean by touching him. Then a Samaritan comes along.

Remember the Jews thought that the Samaritans were not as good as they were. And this is where Jesus puts in a surprise and shock for his listeners! It is the Samaritan who is compassionate. He is the one who goes out of his way to look after the injured man.

This was a great jolt for those who were listening to Jesus. They did not expect that the hero of the story would be the Samaritan. They knew the story was about who belonged in the Kingdom of God. It was a shock to hear Jesus say that the people who were outcasts could be members of God's Kingdom.

Jesus wanted to teach his listeners that the people who belonged to the Kingdom of God were those who were ready to love others and to care for them when they were in need.

(Photo: Bill Thoma

A very important teaching of Jesus is called The Beatitudes. This is how Luke wrote down what Jesus said:

> *Blessed are you who are poor,*
> *for yours is the kingdom of God.*
> *Blessed are you who are hungry now,*
> *for you will be filled.*
> *Blessed are you who weep now,*
> *for you will laugh.*
> **(Luke 6:20–21)**

Jesus is not saying that it is great to be poor or hungry or sad! He is really praising God, who has a special love for those who are weak and in need of help.

When Luke wrote these words down he wanted to explain to his Christians what Jesus meant when he spoke about people being 'poor' or 'rich' in the Kingdom of God.

**52**

The poor of God are the people who know that they need God to help them in their lives. This is easier for people who have no money than for people who are wealthy, because often wealthy people think that their money is what helps them most.

Jesus wanted to teach that rich people can belong to the poor of God if they really believe in Jesus and know that they need God to help them to live good lives; if they do not become rich by treating others unfairly; if they are ready to share their wealth with those who are hungry and in need.

Jesus wanted to teach people in his time that what he did and what he said was bringing the Kingdom of God into everyone's life. The Kingdom of God was for the poor and for the rich people. Only the people who believed that God's Kingdom was happening through Jesus were the poor of God. The rich are the people who do not want to believe that Jesus is God's Word. The rich are those who do not want to change their lives and follow the teachings of Jesus.

Jesus wanted to teach that the Reign of God meant that God always loves and cares for everyone no matter who they are. People can never give back to God as much love as God has for all people. The way to belong to the Kingdom of God is to try to be like God, who is so generous. This means giving generously to other people what they need without expecting them to give back in the same way; forgiving others, even if they do not forgive.

*Jesus did wonderful things for people.*
(Photo: Gordon Flynn)

The teachings of Jesus show him as the Word of God speaking to all people about God's great love and kindness.

But Jesus did not only teach people. We learn about him as God's Word making things happen. Jesus *did* wonderful things for people.

(Photo: Bill Thomas)

# 10 JESUS HEALS AND LIBERATES PEOPLE AS A SIGN OF THE KINGDOM OF GOD

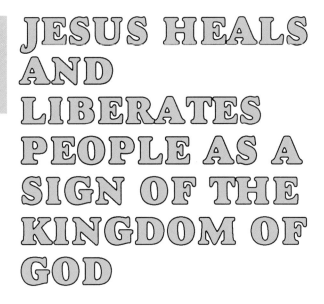

*That evening, at sundown, they brought to him all who were sick or possessed with demons. And the whole city was gathered around the door. And he cured many who were sick with various diseases, and cast out many demons…*
**(Mark 1:32–34)**

*The Power of God working in the lives of people.*
(Photo: Graeme Horner)

T he Gospel writers wanted to tell their Christians about the God whom Jesus revealed. They wanted their Christians to understand that Jesus is the Power of God present in their lives to heal them and liberate them from all their anxieties. To help their Christians understand this, the four Gospel writers gathered together many stories called 'miracle stories'. These stories recalled how Jesus revealed God by the kinds of powerful things Jesus did. They tell how the Reign of God was happening in the lives of the people in Jesus' time.

The miracles tell us so much about who Jesus is and about who God is. The miracles were also *signs* that Jesus had a form of authority and power that no one else had. Jesus had the Power and Authority of God because he is the Word of God.

The miracle stories show that Jesus had power over

- evil spirits
- all kinds of sickness
- death
- nature.

There are many stories in the Gospel that show that Jesus had power over evil spirits. The Gospel words are important clues to tell us about who Jesus is and that he has power to destroy evil.

Mark and Luke tell of a man who had an evil spirit. They both write that the evil spirit in the man said three things to Jesus:

- 'What have you to do with us, Jesus of Nazareth?'
- 'Have you come to destroy us?'
- 'I know you are, the Holy One of God.'
  (Mark 1:24; Luke 4:34)

The evil spirit knew that Jesus of Nazareth is the Holy and chosen One of God who has come to destroy evil in the world.

The miracle story *reveals* that Jesus, as God's Word, wants to destroy evil, and he is the Power of God doing it. He commands the evil spirit,

**56**

## *Be silent, and come out of him!*
### (Mark 1:25–7; Luke 4:35)

Many miracle stories show that Jesus cured crippled people, and those who were blind and deaf, or had any kind of sickness. All these miracles were ways to *reveal* who God is and what God wanted to do for people. They also showed the authority and power of God in Jesus.

One of Jesus' miracles happened in a house in Capernaum. The Synoptic Gospels tell us that there was a great crowd of people listening to Jesus. Some friends of a man who was paralysed wanted Jesus to cure him. They had to break through the roof to reach Jesus. When they reached him he praised the friends for having such great faith in him. Then Jesus turned to the paralysed man and said, 'Take heart, son; your sins are forgiven' (Matthew 9:2

The Scribes and Pharisees were listening and they were shocked that Jesus said this. They were thinking that only God could forgive sins. The Gospels say that Jesus knew what they were thinking. He told them he had the authority to forgive sins, just as he had authority and power to cure the man. Jesus then turned to the man, and said, 'Stand up, take your bed and go to your home.' And the man was cured and was able to walk. The Gospels tell us that the crowd were amazed at this wonderful happening! They could not believe it. This was something they had never seen before, and some of them were afraid. They wondered who this Jesus was.

In this miracle Jesus set the man free in two ways. The man was a captive to his sickness. He could not move. But Jesus also set him free from his sins. It was as if the man was a captive in the power of evil and Jesus set him free. Jesus proved that God's Reign was happening in what he did. When Jesus cured the man's sickness, this was a sign that God's Reign could destroy the power of sin also.

Luke writes the story of a woman whom Jesus cured in the synagogue on the Sabbath. The religious ruler of the synagogue was present at the time.

The woman had a disease that caused her to be bent over. She had this sickness for eighteen years, and in all that time she could not

*Jesus set the man free.*
(Photo: Neil Follett, Scoopix)

straighten her back and walk upright. She had come to pray in the synagogue, and did not even ask Jesus to cure her.

But when Jesus saw how much she suffered, he was filled with compassion for her. He went up to her and said, 'Woman, you are free from your ailment.' Immediately, she could stand up straight and had no more suffering.

The ruler of the synagogue was angry that Jesus had cured the woman on the Sabbath. Jesus knew that the ruler thought the woman was poor, sick and worthless, and that she could come back some other time if she wanted to be cured. Jesus knew, too, that the ruler was challenging the authority of Jesus. It was against the Law of the Sabbath to work on that day. The ruler was the one who had authority to say what the Law meant.

But Jesus had greater authority because Jesus is God's Word. He is more concerned about freeing people from their sickness. This *kind* of miracle *reveals* to us who God is and what God wants most of all. God wants to heal people and set them free from their sins, their sufferings and their fears. God will do this even if people never ask for help. During his life Jesus is the One chosen by God to do this among people.

This miracle also shows that Jesus was full of compassion for those who were sick and cast out from society. Jesus helped them, even if they did not ask him.

The most extraordinary miracles that Jesus did were to raise people from the dead.

Luke writes that one day Jesus saw a funeral in the town of Nain. A young man who was the only son of a widow had died. Jesus knew that the woman was really an outcast in society. Her husband was dead, and without her son to look after her her life would be really very difficult. It was very hard for women in society at that time because no one would care for a woman who had no husband and no son.

Jesus was filled with compassion for her. He knew she had experienced great suffering, and worse suffering would come to her without her son. He went up to her, even though she had not asked for his help.

With great kindness he said to her, 'Do not weep'. He ordered the funeral to stop and turned to where the body was lying. He touched it and said, 'Young man, I say to you, rise.' The dead man sat up and began speaking! Then Jesus gave him back to his mother. Luke writes that the people who saw this were astonished, and they praised God for sending someone so great among them.

Jesus raised the dead man to life to help the mother. The miracle tells us that what Jesus *said* was happening in the Reign of God really *was* happening. God was acting in Jesus to free people, especially those who were most in need of God's help, like this woman. Not even the power of death could be greater than the power of God.

There are many miracle stories in the Synoptic Gospels that show that Jesus had great power over nature. An important story describes how Jesus had power over the wind and the sea.

Jesus' disciples were fishermen. One day he was in the boat with them and they set out to cross the Sea of Galilee. He was tired, so he went to sleep in the boat. Suddenly a strong wind swept down from the mountains across the water. It made great waves in the sea and the boat was rocked from side to side. The disciples in the boat were terrified. They called out to Jesus, 'Teacher, do you not care that we are perishing!' Jesus woke up. He looked out over the water and commanded the wind to stop! Immediately, the wind quietened and the water was calm again. Jesus turned to his disciples and asked them, 'Why are you afraid? Have you still no faith?'

This miracle story shows that Jesus wanted his disciples to believe that when he was with them they would always be safe from anything that could really harm them. To believe in Jesus is the most important part of being in the Kingdom of God.

Each of the Synoptic Gospels say that this caused Jesus' friends to wonder, 'Who then is this, that even the wind and the sea obey him!' (Mark 4:41).

His followers did not know who Jesus was. They had to look for answers too.

*When he was with them they would always be safe from anything that could really harm them.*

(Photo: Author)

(Photo: Helga Leunig)

# 11 JESUS — THE SPECIAL FRIEND OF THE POOR

*… there was a man covered with leprosy. When he saw Jesus, he bowed with his face to the ground and begged him, 'Lord, if you choose, you can make me clean.' Then Jesus stretched out his hand, touched him, and said, 'I do choose. Be made clean.' Immediately the leprosy left him.*
**(Luke 5:12–13)**

*Jesus had a special love for those who suffered in any way.*
(Photo: New York Impressions, copyright Scoopix)

esus had a special love for those who suffered in any way, either because they were poor or hungry, sick or crippled, outcast by society, or oppressed.

In the time of Jesus there were many such people. The poorest of the people could be called the *anawim*. In the time before Jesus the *anawim* were the very poor and needy people of Israel. The *anawim* were the people who had nothing at all to help them. They were cast out by society and the religious authorities. Among these were beggars, sinners, lepers, prostitutes and those possessed by demons. Most of these were called 'unclean', and it was very wrong in the Jewish religion to touch these people. Because they were poor, the wealthy did not care what happened to them. Because they were judged to be 'unclean' by the religious authorities, they were outside the law. They were always the 'losers' in every way. No one cared about them until Jesus came.

There were also crowds of very poor people, who were uneducated, unemployed, sick and crippled, and many women and slaves whose lives were very hard. There seemed no hope for them that any society or religious rules would change to help them. They too were the 'losers' until Jesus came.

The tax-collectors were also outcasts from society. Many of them gathered taxes for the Romans, who had conquered Palestine, so the tax-collectors were often suspected of working with the Romans against the people. They made their own money by demanding more tax money from the people than they needed to pay. This made the people hate the tax-collectors.

During the time of Jesus most of the people in his country were poor and oppressed. Much of the money they earned they paid in taxes. They had to pay taxes on nearly everything they used. This meant that some people, like the rulers, the religious leaders or landowners, became very wealthy. Having wealth gave them great power over the poor people. These powerful, wealthy people thought they were far more important than the poor. The poor suffered because the wealthy and powerful treated them as if they were worthless.

Jesus was exactly the opposite. He loved the poor and had great compassion for them. This did not mean he just felt sorry for them. Instead, he went to the places where they were. He taught them, touched the lepers to cure them, talked with women (it was forbidden for a man to speak to a woman outside her own home). He went among *anawim* and felt in himself how much they suffered. He was then able to understand how they felt, how hard life was for them, how much they struggled, and how hopeless they felt in their lives.

Jesus loved them and treated them with great respect, as an equal with everyone else. He knew that God loved them dearly because they had such great need. They depended on God totally as no one else cared about them.

Jesus loved the poor, but he did not think it was a great thing to be poor. He constantly spoke out against the kinds of rules, especially religious rules, that made life very hard for the poor and suffering people.

One of the things that Jesus did often was to go to the homes of sinners and tax-collectors and have a meal with them. This really shocked the religious leaders and those who were not tax-collectors or sinners. There was a belief in Jesus' time that everyone knew about. The belief was that to share a meal with a person in that person's home was to share in that person's life. When Jesus went to eat with tax-collectors and sinners, it was like sharing their life.

Some people, especially the religious leaders, were horrified that Jesus would share life with these people who were outcasts in society. They thought that if he really was speaking on behalf of God then he should ignore all the *anawim*, the poor, the sinners and the tax-collectors. They said that he could not be the chosen One of God if he continued to eat with these people. Sometimes they jeered Jesus, saying, 'This fellow welcomes sinners and eats with them' (Luke 15:2).

Sometimes the religious rulers complained about Jesus to his disciples. Mark writes that 'When the Scribes and Pharisees saw that he was eating with sinners and tax collectors, they said to his disciples, "Why does he eat with tax collectors and sinners?"' (Mark 2:16).

Jesus always had an answer for them. The answer Jesus gave them was to tell them what the Reign of God is about. Jesus ate with sinners because he wanted to share their lives, and he wanted to show them that their lives were important to God. Jesus challenged the religious rulers to think about the way they treated these outcast people. He told them that these people were precious to God; that they had worth and dignity because God loved them. They were important people in the Kingdom of God.

The Scribes and Pharisees said that these outcast people did not keep the Law. These religious leaders thought that *they* pleased God more by keeping the Law strictly or by paying extra religious taxes. But Jesus claimed that *people* are far more important to God than paying taxes or interpreting the Law the way the religious rulers did. He proclaimed that God was not pleased with *taxes* when the people were left poor and given no justice or mercy. He continually insisted that God's Kingdom means treating people fairly and when they were in need: they should be treated with justice, kindness and mercy.

Jesus' teaching about the Kingdom of God must have been Good News to the poor. Not only did he eat with them in their homes, but he constantly mixed with them, curing their sickness and teaching them that they were precious to God. He continually encouraged them to believe that God loved them and looked after them. They were far more precious to God than the lilies that grew in the fields or the birds in the sky. No one could say that they were worthless, that they were 'non-persons' any more—because they were precious to no less a person than God!

But this was a great challenge to the religious rulers. Jesus wanted them to look inside themselves and see if they were *really* pleasing God in what they were doing. Some of the Pharisees understood what he was challenging them to do, and they changed. But many of them did not change. They did not want to say that other people, especially the *anawim*, the poor, the outcasts, the sinners and the tax-collectors, were as important to God as they were. They did not believe what Jesus was saying. Most times Jesus argued with them when they came to listen to him. In the end they became his enemies.

*'They were far more precious to God than the lilies that grew in the fields or the birds in the sky.'*

(Photo: Helga Leunig)

*'Your Kingdom come…'*
(Photo: Gordon Flynn)

# 12 JESUS CALLS GOD 'ABBA'

*He said to them, 'When you pray, say:*
*Father, hallowed be your name,*
*Your kingdom come...'*
**(Luke 11:2)**

*...God loved them*
*and took care of*
*them even more*
*than a loving*
*parent.*
(Photo: Felicity Hale)

*He said, 'Abba, Father, for you all*
*things are possible;*
*remove this cup from me...'*
**(Mark 14:36)**

There were many Jewish people in the time of Jesus who loved God dearly. For example, Mary, Jesus' mother, must have loved God very much. Both Mary and Joseph were the first people to teach Jesus about God. They taught him that God saved the Israelites from slavery in the past. They taught him that God gave the Law to Moses so that the Israelites would have God's guidance in their lives. He learned that God always remained faithful and loving, even when the Jewish people turned from God.

The Jewish people believed that because God had made a covenant with them, God cared for them in a special way. Many of the Jewish people reverenced God by obeying the Torah. Originally the word Torah was used to describe the whole of the Law that God had given to the chosen people. It is a Hebrew word meaning 'instruction' or 'guidance'.

But by the time of Jesus this written Torah had been surrounded by many other traditions and obligations that made it very difficult for ordinary people to observe God's law as had been originally intended. This meant that God was being removed far beyond any kind of close relationship with the people God cared for in a special way.

But Jesus thought of God in a very different way. He certainly reverenced God by obeying the Torah. But Jesus believed God was really close to people, and especially to him; much closer than anyone could ever believe or imagine.

Jesus loved God more than anyone or anything else. Everything Jesus said and did came from his absolute love for God. He had an intense awareness that God was close with him all the time through his life and especially in his ministry. He always wanted to do what God wanted. The Gospels tell how often Jesus prayed to God. It was as if he could never stop thinking of God and speaking to God. He had a closeness to God that no one else ever had or could ever have. Because he was close to God as no one else was, he described God by a name that was very unusual for a Jew. Jesus described God as 'Abba' ('Father').

Abba is an Aramaic word meaning 'daddy'. 'Abba' and 'Imma' were the first words a little Jewish child learned to call her or his parents. When Jewish children ran into their father's arms they would call out 'Abba'. When they were in their father's arms they knew that they were safe and close to him. They knew that he loved them very much when he held them in his arms and they called him 'Abba'. In the time of Jesus grown-up men and women still called their fathers 'Abba'.

No Jewish person had ever called God 'Abba' in the way Jesus did. When Jesus called God 'Abba', this was something entirely new. It meant that Jesus himself felt total trust in God and was prepared to obey God completely. Jesus believed that God looked after all people the way a mother and father look after their child. He believed that God was truly as loving and as close to people as any parent is to their children.

When he was in agony in the garden of Gethsemane he called out to God, just as a son would call out to his father or mother for help. Jesus cried out in the garden, 'Abba'!

Jesus taught his disciples that God loved them and took care of them even more than a loving parent. He taught them to call God 'Abba' when they prayed to God, and always to know that God was really close to them, and on their side in everything they did. Jesus taught them that because God was 'Abba' to them and to all people, this meant there was a new kind of relationship between them. They were now really brothers and sisters to each other. Because Jesus believed this he taught his disciples to say, *'Our* Father...'

*Slopes of Mt of Olives in the Kidron Valley.*
(Photo: Michael Trainor)

# 13 JESUS AND HIS FOLLOWERS

*He went up the mountain and called to him those whom he wanted, and they came to him. And he appointed twelve, whom he also named apostles, to be with him, and to be sent out to proclaim the message.*
**(Mark 3:13–14)**

*And Jesus said to them, 'Follow me...'*
**(Mark 1:17)**

Jesus was a wonderful person. Crowds followed him, and some people gave up everything they had to be with him. Jesus was a loyal friend. He did not forget about his friends, even when they disappointed him and ran away when he needed them most. He always forgave them and was very patient with them.

There is a different picture of the disciples in each of the Gospels. The Gospel writers wanted to help the Christians of their communities learn how to be a disciple.

The Gospels tell us that there were many crowds who followed Jesus at first. They were amazed at what he taught and at the miracles he performed. From among this crowd some men and women remained as his faithful followers. But the crowd never really stayed loyal to him. They drifted away and left him.

The Gospels also tell us that one of the first things that Jesus did when he began his ministry was to gather together a group of people to be his disciples. He chose many different people: for example some fishermen, Andrew and his brother Simon (whom Jesus named Peter), James and his brother John, a tax-collector called Matthew, and Judas Iscariot (the one who would betray him).

It was not unusual for a Jewish rabbi to have disciples. In the time of Jesus usually a young man who was a disciple went to a rabbi and asked if the rabbi would teach him. The disciple went to the rabbi to gain knowledge so that one day the disciple would be a rabbi.

The disciples of Jesus were different. First, it was *Jesus* who chose them. They must have been really attracted to the personality of Jesus, but *they* did not choose to have him as their rabbi. The Gospels tell us that Jesus said, 'Come, follow me', and they did so straight away without any hesitation.

*'Jesus said, "Come, follow me."'*
(Photo: Scoopix)

Another difference was that Jesus included women among his disciples. No other Jewish rabbi ever did this.

Jesus chose the disciples to have a close friendship with him. That is the most important part of being a disciple of Jesus. To learn a great deal of knowledge is not what is important. Yet Jesus *did* teach them to understand who he was and the importance of his mission to proclaim the Good News of the Kingdom of God.

The disciples of Jesus would always remain his disciples; they would never become rabbis instead of Jesus. Matthew wrote that Jesus said to his disciples: 'But you are not to be called rabbi, for you have one teacher, and you are all students' (Matthew 23:8).

The Synoptic Gospels tell us that Jesus chose twelve men to be a special group among the disciples. In the Israelite religion, Jesus knew that the elected people of God were divided into twelve tribes. These twelve tribes formed the people with whom God had made the special covenant. Jesus knew that God was making a new kind of covenant through what he said and did among the people. Jesus decided to choose twelve men to be the sign that God was electing a new people of God. The twelve were to represent the new covenant with God that was beginning through the ministry of Jesus. Matthew wrote down the names of the twelve (Matthew 10:2).

Jesus did not call his disciples so that they would be just friends with him. He wanted them to learn from him because they were going to play an important part in his ministry for the Kingdom of God. From the time they became his disciples he began to prepare them in a special way to do this. He often took them aside from the crowds and explained his teaching to them very carefully. Mark wrote about this: 'he explained everything in private to his disciples' (Mark 4:33).

In Matthew's Gospel we read that Jesus gave the twelve his own power to go into the villages and countryside and proclaim the Kingdom of God, just as Jesus did. He told them: 'As you go, proclaim the good news, "The kingdom of heaven has come near". Cure the sick, raise the dead, cleanse the lepers, cast out demons' (Matthew 10:7–8).

Luke wrote: 'Soon afterwards he went on through cities and villages, proclaiming and bringing the good news of the kingdom of

God. The twelve were with him as well as some women...Mary called Magdalene and Joanna...and Susanna and many others...' (Luke 8:1–3).

The disciples spent most of their time with Jesus. He loved and trusted them, and shared his mission with them. But the Gospels show that they often argued among themselves about who was the most important among them. They expected Jesus to set up a great Kingdom, and they wanted to be the most important people in it. Jesus had to correct them over and over. The Kingdom of God was not about having power over other people and being important. In Mark's Gospel Jesus told them many times that he was not going to be a great king reigning over people as other kings did. Jesus told them again and again that *his* kingdom was the Kingdom of God. In this Kingdom the poorest of people are important and equal. There is no room in God's Kingdom for anyone who wants to have power over others.

Jesus taught his disciples that proclaiming the Kingdom of God and belonging to it would be hard. He knew that eventually he would have to suffer because *he* proclaimed that the Reign of God was happening in the lives of the people, and the religious rulers did not want him to do this. Jesus warned his disciples that they too would have to suffer for the Kingdom of God. It was a hard lesson for them to learn.

When the time came for Jesus to suffer, most of the disciples were so frightened they ran away and hid themselves. One of them, Judas, betrayed him, and Peter denied ever having anything to do with Jesus. The Gospels tell us that some of the women disciples stayed with Jesus all through his sufferings. They did not understand why he had to suffer, but they loved him and knew that he needed them.

After his resurrection, Jesus came to his disciples. He forgave them for running away, and gave them his own Spirit to be with them when they went out to proclaim the Kingdom of God. They remained faithful to him from then on and all of them *did* suffer as Jesus had told them.

# 14 JESUS DIES ON THE CROSS

*At three o'clock Jesus cried out with a loud voice 'My God, my God, why have you forsaken me?' Then Jesus gave a loud cry and breathed his last.*
**(Mark 15:34, 37)**

Jesus was put to death on a Cross. The story about the death of Jesus is the most important story that the Christians remembered about him.

This is the story of the Passion of Jesus. Each one of the Gospel writers tells this story, but they tell it differently. They wrote about it long after it actually happened. They wrote this story to help the Christians in their churches to understand the meaning of Jesus' death.

*Jesus was put to death on a Cross.*
(Photo: Graeme Horner)

Jesus was put to death because he had made many enemies among the Jewish religious rulers, because of what he said and what he did to proclaim the Kingdom of God. He was condemned to death by Pontius Pilate, the Roman governor, and was executed by the Roman soldiers. He was judged to be a criminal and was crucified on a Cross. This was a common way of putting a criminal to death in that time. Only some of his disciples remained with him when he died.

## Jesus enters Jerusalem

The story of the Passion begins when Jesus went to Jerusalem. He had been there before, but the Gospels tell us that this time he rode a donkey into Jerusalem and many people came out to greet him, praising him and waving palm branches. This had a deep meaning for the Christians, who believed that Jesus was the Messiah. When Jesus went into Jerusalem, he went as the Messiah who was going into his city, Jerusalem, to save people by dying on the Cross.

## Jesus drives the sellers from the Temple

In Jerusalem, Jesus went to the Temple. The Jewish people believed that the Temple was God's holy dwelling place. In the Temple, Jesus found that many people were buying and selling birds and animals. People bought these to offer them to God in the Temple.

Jesus was very angry when he saw this. He did not want God's Holy Temple turned into a market place. He found some rope and made a whip and drove the sellers and the buyers out of the Temple.

When the religious rulers saw this, they were very angry that Jesus would dare to do such a thing. They told him that *they* had authority in the Temple and no one else.

But Jesus was once more showing his authority from God, and they did not want to believe him or want him to challenge their authority.

It made them really determined to have Jesus put to death. Matthew wrote that 'the chief priests and the elders of the people gathered in the palace of the high priest, who was called Caiaphas,

**80**

and they conspired to arrest Jesus by stealth and kill him' (Matthew 26:3–4).

Their plans were helped by Judas Iscariot, who was one of Jesus' disciples. He asked them how much they would give him if he helped them trap Jesus. They offered him thirty pieces of silver, and he agreed to do what they wanted.

*The Last Supper*
(Photo: Graeme Horner)

## The Last Supper

That week the Jews celebrated the Passover feast. During this feast the Jewish people remembered how God had saved them when they were slaves in Egypt. They called this event the Passover or Pasch. A lamb, called the Paschal lamb, was killed, cooked and eaten as part of the feast.

Jesus gathered with his disciples in a friend's house in Jerusalem to celebrate a final meal with them. It was near the day of the Passover feast. All the Gospel writers describe this meal in different ways. We now call this story the story of the Last Supper. Even though the story is different in each Gospel, the four writers wanted their Christians to understand the meaning of what happened during the Last Supper.

All during his ministry Jesus began a new way in which people could be friends with God. Jesus' most important mission was to proclaim that God was saving people through what *he* said and what *he* did. The most important thing that Jesus did was to die on the Cross.

A new 'passover' began with Jesus. When he died on the Cross, he was like the new Paschal Lamb. God saved the Israelites from slavery in Egypt more than a thousand years before. When Jesus died on the Cross, God saved all people in a new way from the slavery of sin and sickness and even death.

It was at the Last Supper that Jesus gave bread and wine to his disciples and said to them to eat the bread and drink the wine. Jesus said, 'This is my body...this is my blood.' He told them to do the same as he had done as a memorial of him. It was in this way that Jesus would be with them always.

## Jesus is in Agony in Gethsemane

When they had eaten the Supper, Jesus went with his friends to the olive garden called Gethsemane. Jesus often went there, especially to pray. On this night he asked his disciples to stay with him, as he was fearful of what would happen to him. They sat down, but soon they fell asleep. Jesus left them and walked farther on to pray to God.

The Gospel writers say that on this night his prayer was different. He was desperately afraid of what was going to happen to him. He knew that everything was possible to God. He called out for help to the God he loved and trusted so much: 'Father, if you are willing, remove this cup from me; yet, not my will but yours be done' (Luke 22:42).

Jesus did not want to suffer and die. He knew that if he was put to death it was because he had taught the people about the Kingdom of God. He believed that God had always loved him and delighted in him. He prayed to God that he would continue to obey God, even if he had to suffer for it. He prayed that he would have the courage to face his enemies and what they might do to him. He was prepared to suffer and die rather than turn away from doing what God had always wanted him to do. Jesus had always taught others to love God more than anything else. In this time of agony for him in Gethsemane he proved that he never failed to do that. He always trusted God, and he continued to trust God even when danger threatened him.

His disciples gave him no comfort in his sorrow. They had fallen asleep. He began to speak to them just as a crowd 'with swords and clubs from the chief priests and elders of the people' came to arrest him. Judas was with them, and when he came close to Jesus he kissed him. This was the sign that Judas had planned with the chief priests and the Scribes. But it is also the sign of friendship, and because Judas used it to betray Jesus, it makes his betrayal of Jesus even more terrible. The guards arrested Jesus and led him away to the palace of the high priest, Caiaphas. His disciples were terrified, and most of them ran away. Peter and another disciple followed Jesus from a distance.

## The Trials of Jesus

The four Gospel writers tell the story of the trials of Jesus. He had two trials. One trial was in front of the Jewish religious rulers. The other trial was in the Roman court.

It was the religious rulers who wanted to put Jesus to death. But the Romans would not allow the Jewish people to execute a public criminal. Only the Romans could do this. The Jewish religious authorities had to make sure that Jesus would be sentenced as a public criminal.

Jesus was arrested in the evening. The Gospels say that he had to wait till early in the morning for his trial before the official religious court, which was called the Sanhedrin.

The Gospels also tell us that during those hours of waiting many of the religious rulers interrogated him. They asked him what he had taught the people about the Kingdom of God and about his great power to work miracles, even though many of them had seen his miracles and heard him teaching people.

The Gospels tell different stories of this time. They tell how Peter followed Jesus into the courtyard of the high priest. Peter was trying to be loyal to Jesus, but he was very frightened that he would be arrested too. It was during this time that Peter denied that he knew anything about Jesus. He even denied that he knew Jesus at all!

All the Gospels say that during this time Jesus was treated harshly, jeered at and tortured. For example, Luke writes: 'Now the men who were holding Jesus began to mock him and beat him; they also blindfolded him and kept asking him, "Prophesy! Who is it that struck you?" They kept heaping many other insults on him' (Luke 22:63–65).

And Mark writes: 'Some began to spit on him, to blindfold him and to strike him…' (Mark 14:65).

Early the next morning, Jesus was led to the Council of the Sanhedrin. This included Pharisees, elders of the people, Scribes and the chief priest. This was the official court that was to condemn Jesus as a criminal who deserved death.

Since Jesus had done nothing that was criminal, the rulers had a problem in finding him guilty. In a court of law, witnesses are needed.

Who would the rulers of the Council bring forward as witnesses? The Gospels say that the Council had to bring *false witnesses* to testify against Jesus, but none of the witnesses could agree on what to say against him.

What could the false witnesses accuse him of doing? The Gospels tell us that they accused him of claiming to destroy the Temple and rebuild it in three days.

But the most important accusation came when the chief priest Caiaphas questioned Jesus. He asked Jesus the meaning of what Jesus had taught the people and what he had done for them.

Then he asked Jesus the last and most important question: 'Are you the Messiah? Are you the Son of God?'

Jesus' life depended on his answer.

What do you think he said when he answered?

Remember that each of the Gospel writers wanted to tell the Christians in their Church that everything that Jesus taught and every miracle he did proved that he was the Messiah, the chosen anointed One of God, the Son of God. Everything he did in his life was God's Word speaking to all people.

We do not know *exactly* what Jesus replied to this question.

In Mark's Gospel, Jesus says, 'I am' and Luke and Matthew write that Jesus says, 'You have said so' or 'You say that I am'.

Jesus at that moment must have believed with all his heart that God had chosen him to carry out God's mission.  He knew that the Messiah was the one chosen by God to do this.  He knew that a Son of God would always do what God wanted, and he knew he had always obeyed God.  He believed that God had anointed him and chosen him to begin God's Reign among people in a new and wonderful way.  He had carried out this mission faithfully in his ministry.

The Gospel writers wanted their Christians to understand that Jesus spoke the truth with the words, 'I am' and 'You say that I am'.

He was the Messiah!  He was the Son of God!

Jesus knew that these rulers in the Council hated him for the way he claimed authority from God to teach and care for all people.  They feared that he would encourage and stir the people to reject the harsh rules and taxes that the rulers placed on the people.

When he answered them, the rulers in the Council were horrified and angry.  They accused him of blasphemy.  They accused him of claiming to have the authority of God!

They looked at him—a man beaten and bruised, standing like a helpless victim in front of them.  How could such a person be the great Messiah, the anointed One of God, specially chosen to carry out God's great mission!

They passed sentence on him:  'He deserves death!' (Matthew 26:66).

They held Jesus as a prisoner, and he was then brought to the Roman court.  Pontius Pilate was governor.  He could free Jesus or sentence him to death.  It depended on what the charges were.

The rulers of the Council were afraid that Pilate might release Jesus if he did not think Jesus was guilty of any crime.  The rulers of the Council knew that Pilate would not think that blasphemy was a crime, because Pilate did not believe in the Jewish religion.  The rulers had to make it seem as if Jesus was a political criminal.  Instead of telling the truth of what had happened in *their* trial of

Jesus, they lied to Pilate. When Pilate asked what crimes Jesus had committed they told him that:

- Jesus was stirring up trouble among the people!
- He was trying to change the laws about taxes, especially taxes paid to the great emperor in Rome!
- He declared that he was the Messiah, which was like being the King of the Jews!

These were serious charges. Pilate questioned Jesus and soon realised that Jesus was innocent of these 'crimes'.

The Gospels tell us that Pilate tried at first to release Jesus, but the chief priests and the elders persuaded the crowd to cry: 'Crucify, crucify him!' (Luke 23:21).

Matthew wrote that Pilate was afraid that a 'riot was beginning' (Matthew 27:24). So, even though Pilate knew that Jesus was innocent, he sentenced him to be flogged and then to be crucified. During this flogging Jesus was mocked as a king. The soldiers put a crown of thorns on his head and a reed in his hand. Then they mocked him, pretending he was a king. They said, 'Hail! King of the Jews!' They spat on him and struck him with the reed.

Jesus carried his own Cross to the place of execution outside the city. It was called Calvary.

There the soldiers nailed him to the Cross, and then lifted it upright. They wrote down on a sign, 'Jesus of Nazareth, King of the Jews'. They wrote this in three languages and nailed it to the Cross over Jesus' head.

Jesus stayed alive for three hours on the Cross. During those three hours many gathered around to mock him and insult him. Among them were the chief priests, Scribes and elders. They really insulted him because they said to him:

*He saved others; he cannot save himself. He is the King of Israel; let him come down from the cross now, and we will believe him. He trusts in God; let God deliver him now, if he wants to; for he said, 'I am God's Son'.* **(Matthew 27:42–43)**

But they would never believe Jesus!  They only wanted to insult him!

When Matthew wrote these words, he wanted his Christians to understand that these words were absolutely true and that the chief priests, Scribes and elders were wrong when they used these words as insults.  Although they were the religious rulers, *they* were the people who did not want to believe who Jesus is and what he does for all people.

Then at three o'clock Jesus cried out in a loud voice, 'My God, my God, why have you forsaken me?' and then he 'breathed his last' breath and died.

### THE HUMAN LIFE OF JESUS ON EARTH HAD COME TO AN END

Mark wrote that when this happened, the centurion soldier who was standing at the foot of the Cross said, 'Truly this man was God's Son!' (Mark 15:39).

The Gospel writers wanted their Christians to understand and believe:

> • That Jesus showed in the way he lived his life that he really is the Son of God.
> • That Jesus showed in the way he lived his life that he really is God's Word revealing who God is and what God is like.
> • That the way he died on the Cross — in great suffering and left alone by everyone, showed that God is very close to all people who suffer in any way:  God shares their sufferings in some mysterious way.

BUT

The resurrection of Jesus shows that God can change suffering so that in some mysterious way suffering is not useless in people's lives. Because of this, Jesus is the Saviour for all people.

# 15 THE RESURRECTION OF JESUS

*Then Jesus said to them, 'Do not be afraid;*
*go and tell my brothers to go to Galilee;*
*there they will see me.'*
**(Matthew 28:10)**

No one saw the resurrection happen. But, even though there were no witnesses to see Jesus rise from the dead, soon after Jesus died his disciples and followers were convinced that he *was* risen and alive and that he was among them again in a new and more wonderful way than before.

When Jesus died on the Cross this *seemed* to be the end of all that Jesus had said and done in his life. The disciples felt saddened and helpless when Jesus died. All their hopes about God's Kingdom continuing in a powerful way on earth came to an end.

The four Gospel writers tell very different stories about the resurrection. In each of the Gospels we read that women went to the tomb of Jesus and found it empty. In Luke's Gospel we read that the women saw two strange men at the tomb who told them that Jesus was not in the tomb. Jesus was risen! The strange men told them to go back to the rest of the disciples. They had to tell the disciples that Jesus was risen and would come to them. The women could not believe what they saw and heard. Mark wrote that they were very frightened.

Then a wonderful thing happened to them. Matthew wrote in his Gospel that Jesus appeared to them! They were so astonished they could not believe that it was possible to see Jesus again.

*He was among them again in a new and more wonderful way than before.*
(Photo: Scoopix: copyright Di Bassett)

Jesus was different. He was not the same as he was before he died. The disciples knew that God had brought about a wonderful change in the body of Jesus. They worshipped Jesus just as they would worship God. Jesus told them to go back to the other disciples to tell them that he was risen and was still with them.

The Gospels tell many stories about the resurrection. The stories tell how the disciples saw Jesus and talked with him. Some of the disciples found it hard to believe that Jesus was risen from the dead. John wrote in his Gospel that Thomas would not believe until he touched the marks of the nails on Jesus' risen body. Jesus came to the disciples when Thomas was there, and then Thomas believed in the risen Jesus.

**90**

The resurrection of Jesus, then, is about having *faith* in him and in his continual presence among Christians.

The resurrection stories tell that the disciples were also 'transformed' in the resurrection of Jesus. They had been frightened and sad after the death of Jesus. The resurrection changed that, because the resurrection is not something that happened for Jesus alone. His resurrection is the way that God continues to be with people, helping them so that they can live their lives in peace and love with others. This changes people's lives. It certainly changed the lives of the disciples.

To help people come to know about this wonderful Good News Jesus came to the disciples in the resurrection and gave his authority to go out and continue to proclaim the Good News of the Kingdom of God just as he had done in his life. Jesus knew that they would not be able to do this by themselves so he promised to be with them always. He promised to give them the Spirit — the Spirit who had been with him during his ministry. The great event of Pentecost is how Luke described the coming of the Spirit.

The resurrection of Jesus is the great event that makes it possible for the Kingdom of God to continue among people from the time of Jesus right until this present time. When he was alive during his ministry, he taught people about the Kingdom of God. He healed people and freed those who were captive to all kinds of sickness and disease. He proclaimed the Good News of God's Reign to the poor and the oppressed. Jesus began a new way in which God would be with all people, which is to last for all time.

He died because he was faithful to this mission. But God would not let that be the end. Jesus is the Word of God, and God continues to speak this Word through all history. The death of Jesus happened in time. The resurrection means that Jesus is risen and can now continue the great mission of God's Kingdom throughout all time.

In the resurrection something wonderful happened to the humanity of Jesus.

We know that if a person seems to die, someone can breathe into them and they can recover. We know that Jesus, before he died, raised people who had died. He raised the widow's son at Nain. But that man would have died again.  There is a great difference between these people being raised from the dead and Jesus' resurrection.

Jesus' resurrection means that God has transformed Jesus and brought him into a new and marvellous kind of life.  Jesus of Nazareth can never die again.  Jesus is now with God, and exalted as the Christ, the Messiah.  It means that God can and will transform the struggles and sufferings of people, even their death.

God cannot be defeated by any kind of suffering, struggle, fear, threat of disaster of any kind.  God transforms all these into the possibility of giving people freedom and happiness.

In the death of Jesus, God has destroyed all that can cause harm to people.

No one needs to be afraid or to worry, because Jesus has brought the Kingdom of God into the world.

A new kind of life for all people has begun with the Resurrection of Jesus!

*God transforms all these into the possibility of giving people freedom and happiness.*
(Photo: Helga Leunig)

# THE BIBLE - GOD'S WORD

## LAURIE WOODS

*The Bible - God's Word* has been designed as a resource book for use in upper primary and lower secondary schools. This full-colour publication covers a wide selection of topics that are key issues in the study of the Bible. It examines questions such as: What is the Bible? How did the Bible authors know what to write? How did the Bible get here? How did it get its name?

Concepts such as Truth in Genesis, Messiah, Book of Exodus and Moses and the Law are easily explained. It also examines books of both the Hebrew and Christian Bible.

**ISBN 1 86371 154 6**

# COLLINS DOVE DICTIONARY
# FOR YOUNG CATHOLICS
## EDITED BY LAURIE WOODS

This dictionary presents information about the theology, scripture, history and liturgy of the Catholic church.

It contains over 800 words and definitions from the Catholic tradition.

The language and information given is suitable for upper primary and lower secondary students.

It provides information about Bible characters, The Books of the Old and New Testament.

**ISBN 0 85924 736 8**

**RELATED TITLES:**

# WE BELIEVE

*Prayers, Readings and Stories for Young Catholics*

MATT McDONALD

ANN BENJAMIN

A superb reference for junior secondary students.

Presented in wonderful full-colour *We Believe* is an anthology featuring the beliefs, stories, prayers and liturgy of the Catholic tradition.

*We Believe* is:

- a valuable summary of Catholicism

- an excellent confirmation gift

- a valuable class set reference for secondary schools

- a handy resource for RCIA classes along with *Understanding Catholicism*

- Contains full-colour photographs

- Compares and closely analyses biblical references

- Studies the many and varied ways in which we interpret, the Bible, the image of Christ, the role of the church and the place of the sacraments.

ISBN 0 85924 737 6